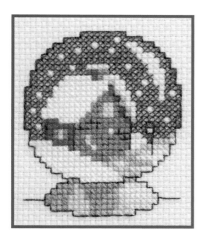

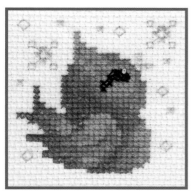

50
cross stitch
QUICKIES
CHRISTMAS

For over a century, Bucilla has delivered beautiful holiday needlecrafts that are a pleasure to stitch and a treasure for generations to enjoy. Our seasonal Christmas collection of quick and easy cross stitch continues with these fifty designs.

These miniature stitchery designs are quick to make for decorations and gifts. This fun collection represents a large variety of themes, from Santas and snowmen to angels and trees. Finishing ideas begin on page 31.

Visit our website to share in the joy of creating beautiful Bucilla stitched pieces.

PLAID
Bucilla®

LEISURE ARTS, INC. • Maumelle, Arkansas

Angel with Crosses

Stitch Count: 27w x 31h
Design Size: 2" x 2¼" on 14 count white Aida

Cross Stitch-2 strands

☆	743	yellow
~	818	lt pink
♥	666	red
✿	498	dk red
+	907	lt green
H	904	green
=	519	lt blue

Backstitch-1 strand

╱	498	dk red
╱	782	gold
╱	798	blue
╱	890	dk green
╱	904	green
╱	938	brown

Straight Stitch-2 strands

╱	782	gold

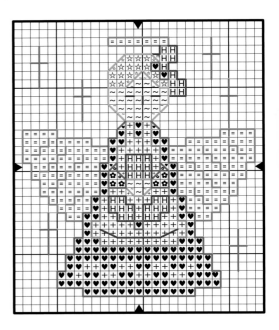

Angel with Trumpet

Stitch Count: 25w x 34h
Design Size: 1⅞" x 2½" on 14 count white Aida

Cross Stitch-2 strands

◇	948	lt pink
⊠	3706	pink
✿	3801	dk pink
♥	321	red
✳	725	yellow
⊞	782	gold
⌃	775	lt blue
⊡	3325	blue
=	3827	lt brown

Backstitch

╱	300	brown-2 strands
╱	300	brown-1 strand
╱	3799	grey-1 strand

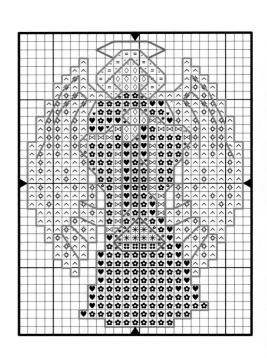

Away in a Manger

Stitch Count: 34w x 35h
Design Size: 2½" x 2½" on 14 count white Aida

Cross Stitch-2 strands

◊	948	lt pink
✳	725	dk yellow
▣	783	lt gold
▦	782	gold
∧	775	lt blue
=	3854	lt orange
◉	3776	rust
⊠	300	dk rust
⊡	blanc	white

Backstitch-1 strand

╱	322	blue
╱	300	dk rust

French Knot-2 strands

●	322	blue

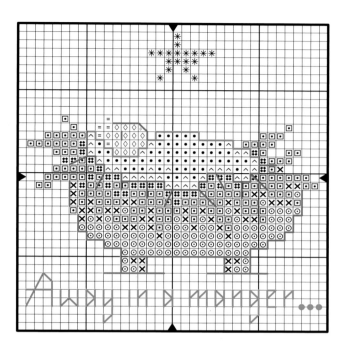

Baby's 1st Christmas

Stitch Count: 30w x 30h
Design Size: 2⅛" x 2⅛" on 14 count white Aida

Cross Stitch-2 strands

∧	775	lt blue
4	964	lt aqua
⊠	962	pink
➡	959	aqua
▼	3799	grey
⊡	blanc	white

Backstitch-1 strand

╱	3812	aqua
╱	962	pink
╱	3799	grey
╱	813	blue

French Knot-2 strands

●	962	pink
●	3812	aqua

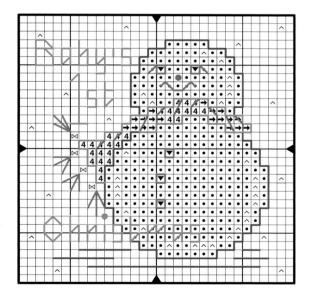

Candle

Stitch Count: 34w x 31h
Design Size: 2½" x 2¼" on 14 count white Aida

Cross Stitch-2 stands

⋈	3706	pink
✿	3705	dk pink
♥	321	red
☆	745	lt yellow
÷	726	yellow
✳	725	dk yellow
⊡	783	gold
🐞	320	green
♠	367	dk green

Backstitch-1 strand

/	3799	grey

French Knot-2 strands

●	725	dk yellow

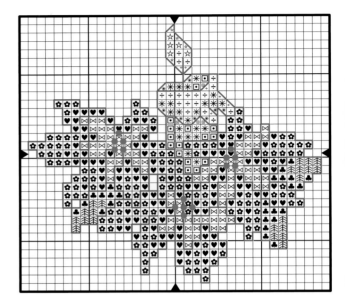

Candy Cane

Stitch Count: 33w x 34h
Design Size: 2⅜" x 2½" on 14 count white Aida

Cross Stitch-2 strands

⊞	3708	lt pink
⋈	3706	pink
✿	3801	dk pink
♥	321	red
P	368	lt green
🐞	320	green
▽	367	dk green
⌃	775	blue
⊡	blanc	white

Backstitch-1 strand

/	304	dk red
/	367	dk green

French Knot-2 strands

●	367	dk green

Cardinal

Stitch Count: 28w x 28h
Design Size: 2" x 2" on 14 count white Aida

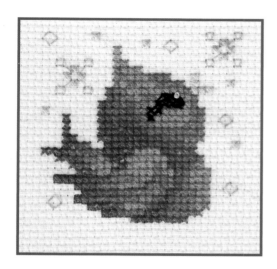

Cross Stitch-2 strands

★	3820	yellow
⌂	3801	pink
⊞	666	lt red
♡	321	red
◆	304	dk red
✳	3325	blue
✚	310	black

Backstitch-1 strand

╱	498	vy dk red
╱	3325	blue
╱	310	black

French Knot-2 strands

●	blanc	white

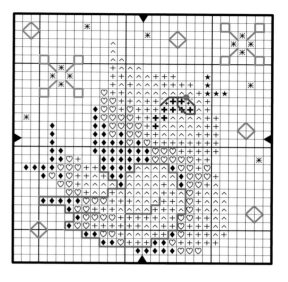

Chimney Santa

Stitch Count: 37w x 36h
Design Size: 2¾" x 2⅝" on 14 count white Aida

Cross Stitch-2 strands

U	950	peach
⋈	3706	pink
✿	3705	lt red
♥	321	red
✳	725	yellow
▣	783	gold
P	368	lt green
★	320	green
✺	367	dk green
⌃	775	lt blue
⊞	322	blue
⩵	3855	lt yellow
⊠	400	brown
▼	414	grey
■	310	black
⊡	blanc	white

Backstitch-1 strand

╱	304	dk red
╱	367	dk green
╱	322	blue
╱	400	brown
╱	310	black

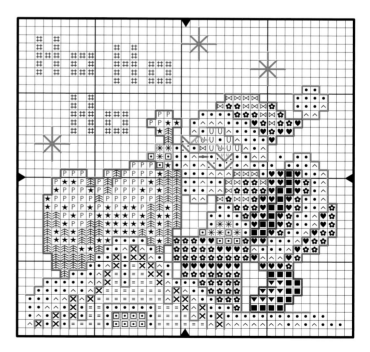

Christmas Tree

Stitch Count: 29w x 35h
Design Size: 2⅛" x 2½" on 14 count white Aida

Cross Stitch-2 strands

◎	3804	pink
♥	666	red
⊞	907	lt green
H	904	green
▣	434	lt brown
⊡	blanc	white
=	519	blue-1 strand

Backstitch-1 strand

/	498	dk red
/	904	green
/	890	dk green
/	898	brown

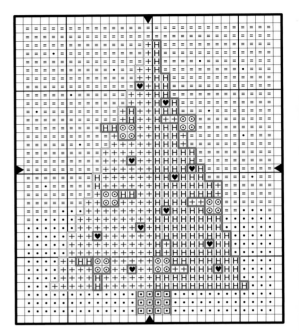

Christmas Wreath

Stitch Count: 28w x 28h
Design Size: 2" x 2" on 14 count white Aida

Cross Stitch-2 strands

⊞	3801	pink
◆	321	red
S	164	lt green
#	989	green
⊡	blanc	white

Backstitch-1 strand

/	310	black

French Knot-2 strands

●	blanc	white

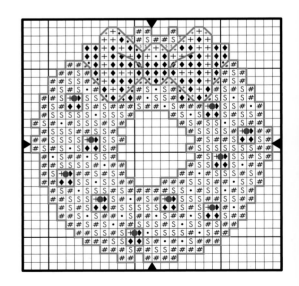

Gingerbread House

Stitch Count: 30w x 29h
Design Size: 2¼" x 2⅛" on 14 count white Aida

Cross Stitch-2 strands

♥	321	red
✳	725	yellow
▽	702	green
▣	3823	lt yellow
◎	3776	rust
☒	975	brown
·	blanc	white

Backstitch-1 strand

/	321	red
/	702	green
/	322	blue
/	3799	grey
/	blanc	white

French Knot-2 strands

●	3799	grey

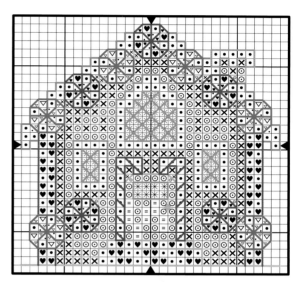

Gnome

Stitch Count: 29w x 35h
Design Size: 2⅛" x 2½" on 14 count white Aida

Cross Stitch-2 strands

ᨆ	818	pink
♥	666	red
⊞	907	lt green
H	904	green
■	310	black
·	blanc	white
ᴧ	597	blue-1 strand

Backstitch-1 strand

/	498	dk red
/	890	dk green
/	318	grey
/	310	black

Straight Stitch-2 strands

/	blanc	white

French Knot-2 strands

●	310	black
●	blanc	white

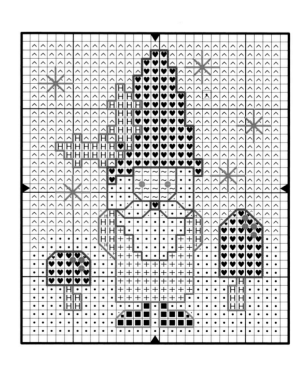

Happy Howl-a-days

Stitch Count 35w x 33h
Design Size: 2½" x 2⅜" on 14 count white Aida

Cross Stitch-2 strands

◇	948	peach
✿	3801	lt red
♥	321	red
▫	745	lt yellow
✳	725	yellow
=	977	rust
◎	976	lt brown
✕	300	brown
∧	775	lt blue
■	310	black
•	blanc	white

Backstitch-1 strand

╱	304	dk red
╱	322	blue
╱	3799	grey

French Knot-2 strands

●	3799	grey

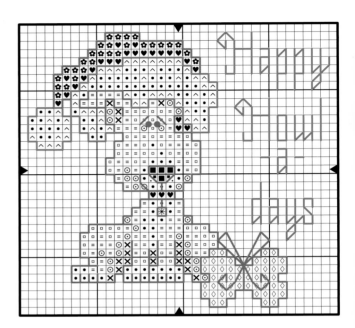

Holiday Ornaments

Stitch Count: 27w x 34h
Design Size: 2" x 2½" on 14 count white Aida

Cross Stitch-2 strands

♥	666	red
⊞	907	lt green
Ⓐ	906	green
Ⓗ	904	dk green
■	310	black
▫	blanc	white

Backstitch-1 strand

╱	498	dk red
╱	904	dk green
╱	890	vy dk green
╱	310	black
╱	blanc	white

French Knot-2 strands

●	666	red

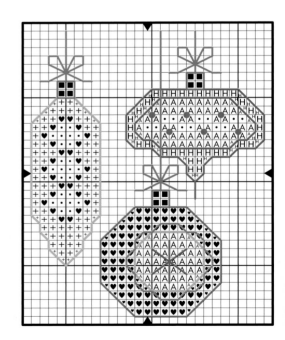

Joyful Santa

Stitch Count: 29w x 34h

Design Size: 2⅛" x 2½" on 14 count white Aida

Cross Stitch-2 strands

☆	743	yellow
~	818	pink
♥	666	red
H	904	green
■	310	black
·	blanc	white

Backstitch-1 strand

/	498	dk red
/	890	dk green
/	414	grey
/	310	black

Straight Stitch-2 strands

/	597	blue

French Knot-2 strands

●	310	black

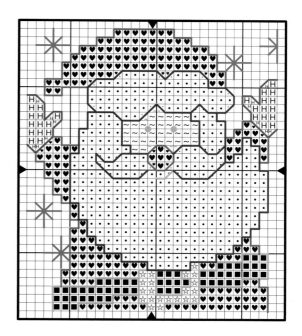

Kitty

Stitch Count: 27w x 28h

Design Size: 2" x 2" on 14 count white Aida

Cross Stitch-2 strands

▫	3801	pink
✕	666	red
♥	321	dk red
T	437	tan
▼	435	dk tan
◪	434	brown
■	310	black
·	blanc	white

Backstitch-1 strand

/	3820	yellow
/	367	green
/	310	black

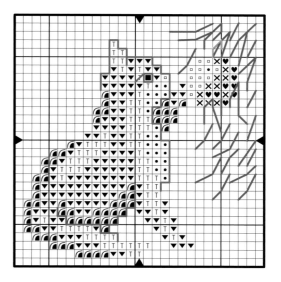

Let It Snow

Stitch Count: 25w x 31h

Design Size: 1⅞" x 2¼" on 14 count white Aida

Cross Stitch-2 strands

⊠ 3846 blue

Backstitch-1 strand

╱ 907 lt green

╱ 700 green

╱ 321 red

╱ 602 pink

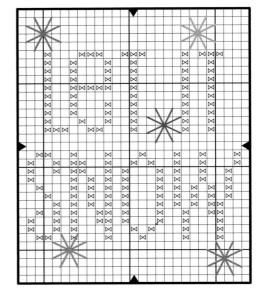

Merry Christmas

Stitch Count: 34w x 35h

Design Size: 2½" x 2½" on 14 count white Aida

Cross Stitch-2 strands

☆ 745 lt yellow

✳ 725 yellow

P 368 lt green

▤ 320 green

◙ 976 rust

⊠ 975 brown

Backstitch-1 strand

╱ 367 dk green

╱ 975 brown

French Knot-2 strands

● 304 red

● 367 dk green

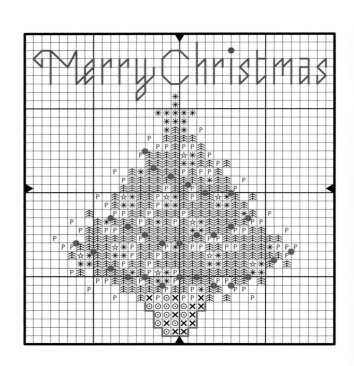

Mitten

Stitch Count: 28w x 28h
Design Size: 2" x 2" on 14 count white Aida

Cross Stitch-2 strands

✿	3801	pink
S	321	red
♥	304	dk red
⊡	blanc	white

Backstitch-1 strand

╱	blanc	white
╱	300	brown
╱	598	blue

Modern Reindeer

Stitch Count: 29w x 35h
Design Size: 2⅛" x 2½" on 14 count white Aida

Cross Stitch-2 strands

♥	321	red
◇	905	green
⊠	975	brown
■	310	black
⊡	blanc	white
⌃	3846	blue-1 strand

Backstitch-1 strand

╱	310	black
╱	blanc	white
╱	905	green
╱	907	lt green

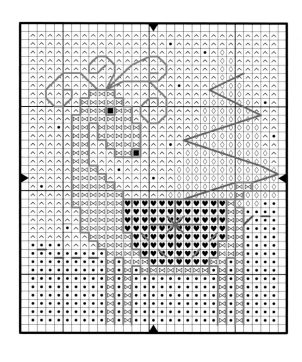

Nativity

Stitch Count: 33w x 33h
Design Size: 2⅜" x 2⅜" on 14 count white Aida

Cross Stitch-2 strands

◇	948	lt peach
U	950	peach
P	368	lt green
▦	320	green
⌃	775	lt blue
⊞	3325	blue
⊞	322	dk blue
⊡	745	yellow
☒	300	brown
⊡	blanc	white

Backstitch

╱	725	dk yellow-2 strands
╱	322	dk blue-1 strand
╱	3799	grey-1 strand

French Knot-2 strands

●	322	dk blue

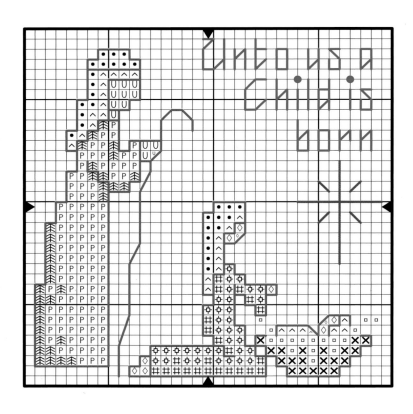

Mr. Snowman

Stitch Count: 29w x 35h

Design Size: 2⅛" x 2½" on 14 count white Aida

Cross Stitch-2 strands

♥	321	red
⊞	971	orange
H	906	green
⊡	434	brown
▼	318	grey
■	310	black
·	blanc	white
◇	799	blue-1 strand

Backstitch-1 strand

╱	498	dk red
╱	890	dk green
╱	310	black

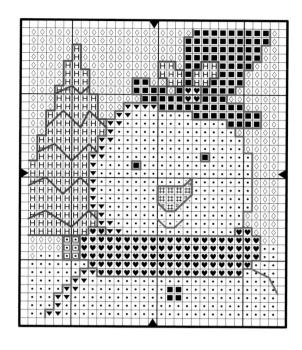

Noel

Stitch Count: 33w x 34h

Design Size: 2⅜" x 2½" on 14 count white Aida

Cross Stitch-2 strands

#	743	yellow
★	742	dk yellow
✕	321	red
S	954	vy lt green
⌂	912	lt green
♣	910	green
¢	3325	blue
▫	blanc	white

Backstitch-1 strand

╱	742	dk yellow
╱	321	red
╱	3818	dk green
╱	535	grey

French Knot-2 strands

●	742	dk yellow

Lazy Daisy Stitch-2 strands

⟃	742	dk yellow

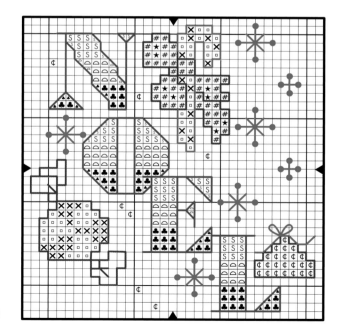

Noel Squared

Stitch Count: 31w x 31h
Design Size: 2¼" x 2¼" on 14 count white Aida

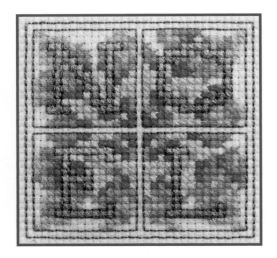

Cross Stitch-2 strands

★	725	yellow
⊡	3708	lt pink
⌃	3706	pink
♡	3801	dk pink
◆	321	red
▫	3817	vy lt green
A	3816	lt green
$	163	dk green

Backstitch-1 strand

╱	561	vy dk green

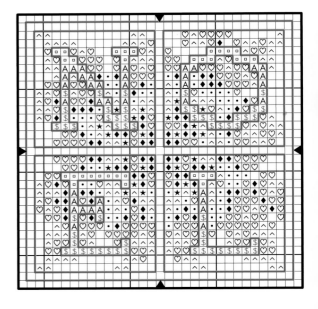

Nordic Reindeer

Stitch Count: 35w x 34h
Design Size: 2½" x 2½" on 14 count white Aida

Cross Stitch-2 strands

⊠	321	red
☾	415	grey
⊡	436	tan
⊞	434	lt brown
⌐	912	lt green
$	700	green

Backstitch-1 strand

╱	433	brown
╱	498	dk red
╱	535	dk grey
╱	700	green
╱	813	blue

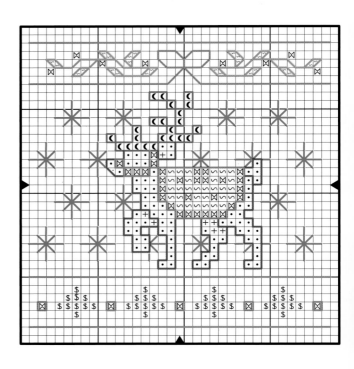

Nutcracker

Stitch Count 15w x 34h
Design Size: 1⅛" x 2½" on 14 count white Aida

Cross Stitch-2 strands

U	950	peach
+	605	pink
✿	3801	dk pink
♥	321	red
☆	745	lt yellow
✳	725	yellow
⊞	322	blue
+	803	dk blue
⌘	317	grey
▼	3799	dk grey
■	310	black
⊡	blanc	white

Backstitch-1 strand

╱	310	black

French Knot-2 strands

●	725	yellow

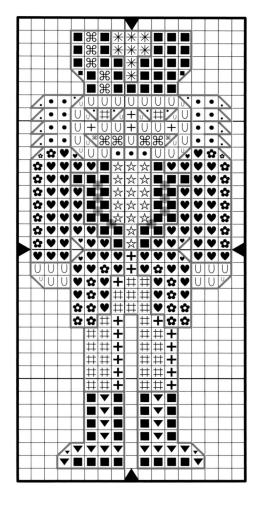

15

Ornaments

Stitch Count: 33w x 32h
Design Size: 2⅜" x 2⅜" on 14 count white Aida

Cross Stitch-2 strands

⊠	894	pink
✿	666	red
♥	304	dk red
☆	745	lt yellow
÷	726	yellow
✳	725	dk yellow
⊡	783	gold
⊞	782	dk gold
P	368	lt green
⧉	320	green
▽	367	dk green
⊡	blanc	white

Backstitch-1 strand

╱	782	dk gold
╱	304	dk red
╱	3799	grey

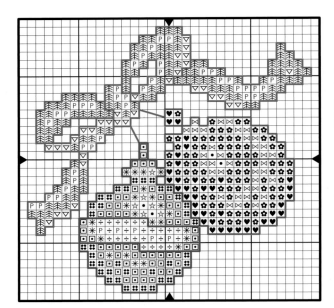

Panda

Stitch Count: 22 x 28
Design Sizes: 1⅝" x 2" on 14 count white Aida

Cross Stitch-2 strands

⌘	413	grey
▼	3799	dk grey
℮	369	lt green
P	368	green
⧉	367	dk green
✛	3705	pink
✿	666	red
♥	304	dk red
■	310	black
⊡	blanc	white

Backstitch-1 strand

╱	3705	pink
╱	blanc	white
╱	310	black

French Knot-2 strands

●	blanc	white

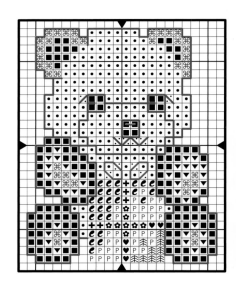

Peace Dove

Stitch Count: 36w x 30h
Design Size: 2⅝" x 2¼" on 14 count white Aida

Cross Stitch-2 strands

☆	745	yellow
⊞	320	green
⊡	blanc	white
⌂	775	lt blue

Backstitch-1 strand

∕	320	green
∕	322	blue
∕	318	grey

French Knot-2 strands

●	322	blue

Peace on Earth

Stitch Count: 25w x 29h
Design Size: 1⅞" x 2⅛" on 14 count white Aida

Cross Stitch-2 strands

♥	666	red
✿	498	dk red
A	906	lt green
H	904	green
■	310	black

Backstitch

╱	666	red-2 strands
╱	906	lt green-2 strands
╱	498	dk red-1 strand
╱	890	dk green-1 strand
╱	310	black-1 strand

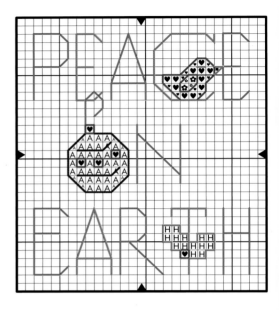

Penguin with Bell

Stitch Count: 27w x 26h
Design Size: 2" x 1⅞" on 14 count white Aida

Cross Stitch-2 strands

∼	3822	yellow
O	3852	dk yellow
▫	3801	lt red
+	666	red
△	304	dk red
◆	498	vy dk red
#	3761	lt blue
■	310	black
·	blanc	white

Backstitch-1 strand

╱	3852	dk yellow
╱	3801	lt red
╱	498	vy dk red
╱	597	blue
╱	310	black

French Knot-2 strands

●	blanc	white

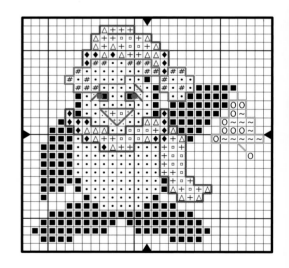

Penguin with Banner

Stitch Count: 34w x 36h
Design Size: 2½" x 2⅝" on 14 count white Aida

Cross Stitch-2 strands

♥	321	red
▽	702	green
⊙	976	orange
^	775	lt blue
▼	3799	dk grey
■	310	black
•	blanc	white

Backstitch-1 strand

╱	322	dk blue
╱	310	black

French Knot-2 strands

●	322	dk blue
●	310	black

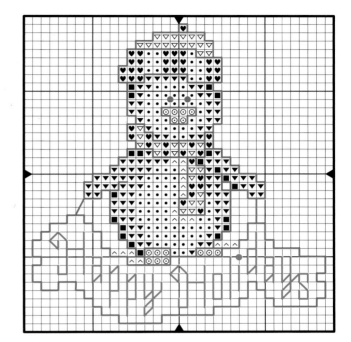

Penguin's Gift

Stitch Count: 29w x 35h
Design Size: 2⅛" x 2½" on 14 count white Aida

Cross Stitch-2 strands

♥	666	red
⊞	3853	orange
✦	907	lt green
✕	310	black
•	blanc	white
⊞	907	lt green-1 strand
H	904	green-1 strand

Backstitch-1 strand

╱	498	dk red
╱	904	green
╱	310	black

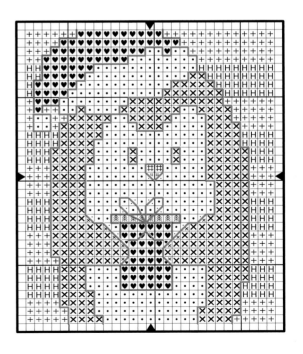

Pinecones & Candles

Stitch Count 26w x 28h
Design Size: 1⅞" x 2" on 14 count white Aida

Cross Stitch-2 strands

⌣	436	lt brown
Ⓜ	434	brown
⊠	702	lt green
♣	699	green
⊡	415	grey
⊡	blanc	white
★	743	yellow
J	741	orange
O	321	red

Backstitch-1 strand

╱	535	dk grey
╱	741	orange
╱	699	green
╱	321	red

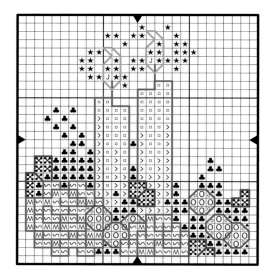

Poinsettia

Stitch Count: 34w x 32h
Design Size: 2½" x 2⅜" on 14 count white Aida

Cross Stitch-2 strands

⊠	894	pink
✿	3705	red
♥	304	dk red
⊡	783	gold
P	368	lt green
圂	320	green

Backstitch-1 strand

╱	3799	dk grey

Presents

Stitch Count: 27w x 27h

Design Size: 2" x 2" on 14 count white Aida

Cross Stitch-2 strands

⊡	3801	vy lt red
⊠	666	lt red
♥	321	red
⏣	304	dk red
=	369	vy lt green
⊞	368	lt green
♣	320	green
◆	367	dk green

Backstitch-1 strand

╱	3801	vy lt red
╱	367	dk green
╱	3821	gold

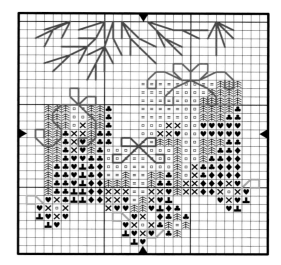

Puppy

Stitch Count: 28w x 28h

Design Size: 2" x 2" on 14 count white Aida

Cross Stitch-2 strands

⊡	3801	lt red
♥	321	red
T	437	lt tan
⊞	436	tan
▼	435	dk tan
◪	434	lt brown
◨	433	brown
■	310	black
⊡	blanc	white

Backstitch-1 strand

╱	3347	green
╱	310	black

French Knot-2 strands

●	blanc	white

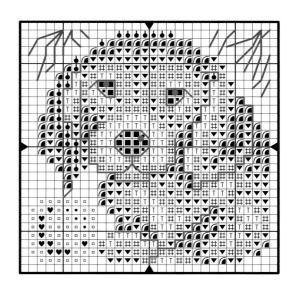

Reindeer

Stitch Count: 29w x 35h
Design Size: 2⅛" x 2½" on 14 count white Aida

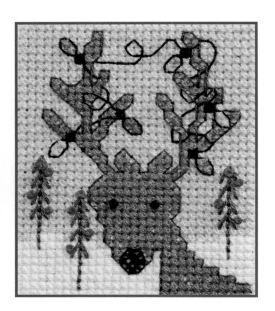

Cross Stitch-2 strands

☆	444	yellow
◇	3805	pink
♥	666	red
⊞	907	lt green
⊡	434	lt brown
■	310	black
⊡	blanc	white
⊟	519	blue-1 strand

Backstitch

╱	904	green-2 strands
╱	898	brown-1 strand
╱	310	black-1strand

French Knot-2 strands

●	666	red
●	310	black

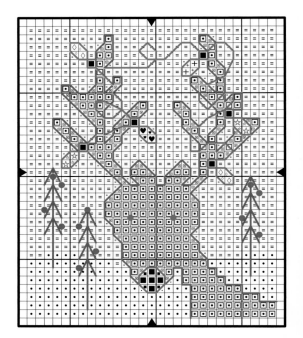

Rocking Horse

Stitch Count: 32w x 32h
Design Size: 2⅜" x 2⅜" on 14 count white Aida

Cross Stitch-2 strands

♥	304	red
P	368	lt green
▽	702	green
✿	803	blue
▫	3823	yellow
⊟	977	rust
◎	976	lt brown
✕	300	brown

Backstitch-1 strand

╱	3799	grey

French Knot-2 strands

●	304	red

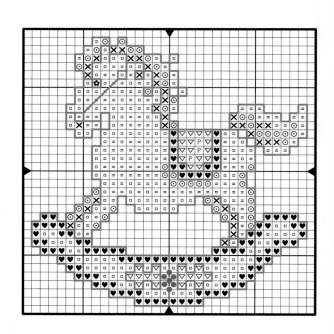

Rudy

Stitch Count: 27w x 28h
Design Size: 2" x 2" on 14 count white Aida

Cross Stitch-2 strands

✿	666	red
♥	304	dk red
⁄	762	lt grey
3	415	grey
=	738	lt brown
◎	436	brown
☒	435	dk brown
■	310	black
⊡	blanc	white

Backstitch-1 strand

╱	304	dk red
╱	310	black

French Knot-2 strands

●	blanc	white

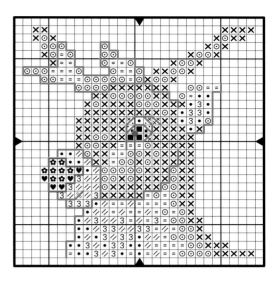

Santa & Snowman

Stitch Count: 35w x 35h
Design Size: 2½" x 2½" on 14 count white Aida

Cross Stitch-2 strands

⊍	950	peach
⊠	3706	pink
✿	3801	dk pink
♥	321	red
✳	725	yellow
P	368	lt green
▽	702	green
⌃	775	vy lt blue
⊞	334	lt blue
✚	803	dk blue
⊟	977	rust
⌘	317	grey
▼	3799	dk grey
■	310	black
⊡	blanc	white

Backstitch-1 strand

╱	304	dk red
╱	300	brown
╱	322	blue
╱	803	dk blue
╱	310	black

French Knot-2 strands

●	310	black

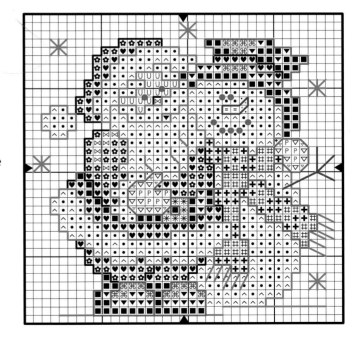

Santa's Sleigh

Stitch Count: 34w x 34h

Design Size: 2½" x 2½" on 14 count white Aida

Cross Stitch-2 strands

⊠	3706	pink
✿	3801	dk pink
♥	321	red
✳	725	yellow
⊡	783	gold
⊞	782	dk gold
P	368	lt green
⊠	320	green
A	367	dk green

Backstitch-1 strand

╱	782	dk gold
╱	367	dk green
╱	322	blue
╱	3799	dk grey
╱	317	grey-2 strands

French Knot-2 strands

●	367	dk green

Season's Greetings

Stitch Count: 33w x 33h

Design Size: 2⅜" x 2⅜" on 14 count white Aida

Cross Stitch-2 strands

⌧	3706	pink
✿	3801	dk pink
♥	321	red
P	368	lt green
▽	320	green
⎕	367	dk green

Backstitch-1 strand

╱	367	dk green

French Knot-2 strands

●	367	dk green

Snow Globe

Stitch Count: 28w x 34h

Design Size: 2" x 2½" on 14 count white Aida

Cross Stitch-2 strands

★	744	lt yellow
÷	726	yellow
✳	725	dk yellow
⊡	783	lt gold
⊞	782	gold
✿	3801	lt red
♥	321	red
⎕	320	green
=	977	tan
⌃	775	lt blue
⊕	3325	blue
·	blanc	white
⌘	317	lt grey
?	803	dk blue-1 strand

Backstitch-1 strand

╱	3799	grey

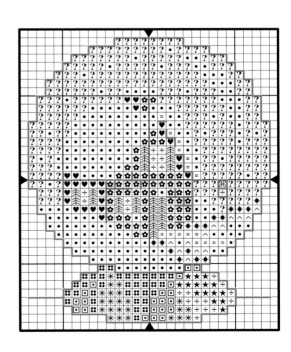

Snowflake

Stitch Count: 35w x 35h
Design Size: 2½" x 2½" on 14 count white Aida

Cross Stitch-2 strands
⌃ 775   lt blue
⊞ 3325   blue
Backstitch-1 strand
╱ 322   dk blue

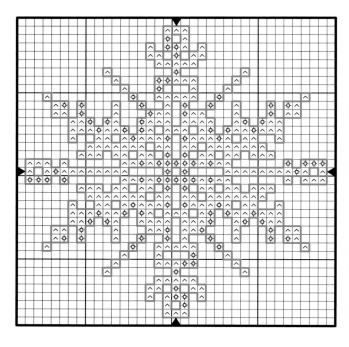

Stocking

Stitch Count: 23w x 26h
Design Size: 1¾" x 1⅞" on 14 count white Aida

Cross Stitch-2 strands
⌃ 747   lt blue
⊠ 3801   lt red
✿ 666   red
♥ 321   dk red
⊡ blanc   white
Backstitch-1 strand
╱ 807   blue

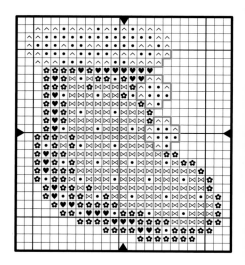

Snowman

Stitch Count: 34w x 35h
Design Size: 2½" x 2½" on 14 count white Aida

Cross Stitch-2 strands

⌂	775	lt blue
⊞	322	blue
⊞	803	dk blue
⊟	3827	orange
⊠	300	brown
⌘	317	grey
■	310	black
⊡	blanc	white

Backstitch-1 strand

╱	803	dk blue
╱	310	black
╱	322	blue

French Knot-2 strands

●	803	dk blue
●	310	black

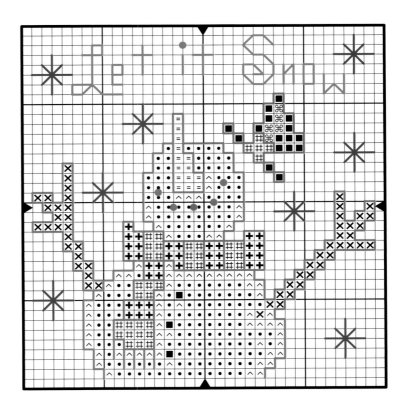

Skaters

Stitch Count: 36w x 28h
Design Size: 2⅝" x 2" on 14 count white Aida

Cross Stitch-2 strands

U	950	peach
⋈	3706	pink
✿	3705	dk pink
✳	725	yellow
▽	702	yellow-green
✥	320	green
∧	775	vy lt blue
⊕	3325	lt blue
⊞	334	blue
✛	803	dk blue
◉	976	rust
Y	414	grey

Backstitch-1 strand

╱	334	blue
╱	3799	dk grey

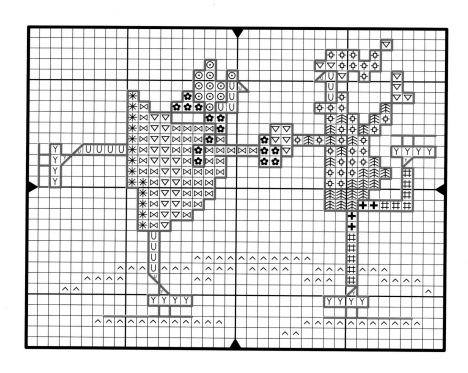

Winter Wishes

Stitch Count: 29w x 35h
Design Size: 2⅛" x 2½" on 14 count white Aida

Cross Stitch-2 strands

♥	666	red
■	310	black
·	blanc	white
◊	519	lt blue-1 strand

Backstitch

/	798	blue-1 strand
/	498	dk red-1 strand
/	317	grey-1 strand
/	310	black-1 strand
/	906	lt green-2 strands
/	904	green-2 strands

French Knot-2 strands

●	798	blue
●	310	black

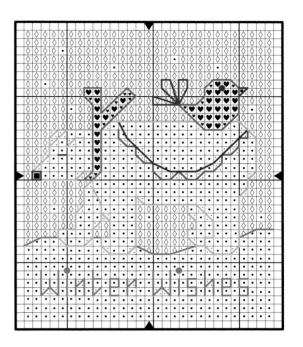

Wreath

Stitch Count: 30w x 34h
Design Size: 2⅛" x 2½" on 14 count white Aida

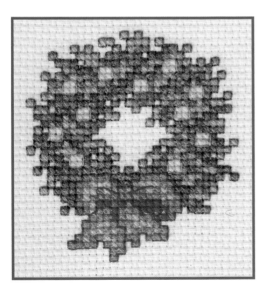

Cross Stitch-2 strands

⋈	894	pink
✿	3705	red
♥	304	dk red
☆	745	lt yellow
✳	725	yellow
P	368	lt green
⧖	320	green
▲	367	dk green

Backstitch-1 strand

/	304	dk red
/	783	dk yellow
/	367	dk green

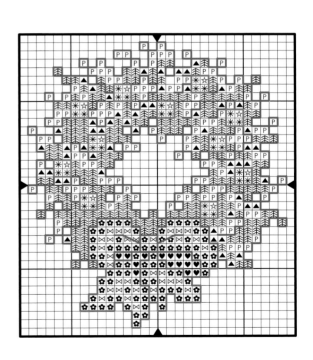

General Instructions

HOW TO READ CHARTS

Each design is made up of a key and a charted pattern on which each square represents a stitch. The symbols in the key indicate which floss color to use for each stitch on the chart. The key will indicate the stitch and how many strands of floss to use.

 A square filled with a full-size symbol should be stitched as a **Cross Stitch**.

 A reduced symbol in a corner of the square is usually stitched as a **One-Quarter Stitch**. When a Backstitch crosses two squares and a reduced symbol is in a corner of the square, a **Three-Quarter Stitch** is performed.

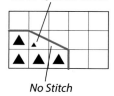

Three-Quarter Stitch

No Stitch

 A straight line should be stitched as a **Backstitch**.

 A large dot should be stitched as a **French Knot**.

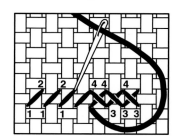 An oval should be stitched as a **Lazy Daisy Stitch**.

Sometimes the symbol for a Cross Stitch will be on either side of a Backstitch line. Other times the symbol for a Cross Stitch will be partially covered when a Backstitch, French Knot, or Lazy Daisy Stitch crosses that square.

GETTING STARTED

Preparing Fabric

Cut your fabric at least 3" larger on all sides than the design and overcast the edges to keep from fraying. It is better to waste a little fabric than to come up short after many hours of stitching.

Working with Floss

To ensure smoother stitches, separate floss into individual strands; then, realign them before threading the needle. Keep stitching tension consistent. Begin and end floss by running under several stitches on the back; never tie knots.

Where to Start

The horizontal and vertical centers of each charted design are shown by arrows. You may start at any point on the charted design, but be sure the design will be centered on the fabric. Locate the center of the fabric by folding it in half, top to bottom and again left to right. On the charted design, count the number of squares (stitches) from the center of the chart to where you wish to start. Then, from the fabric's center, find your starting point by counting out the same number of fabric threads (stitches).

HOW TO STITCH

Always work Cross Stitches, One-Quarter Stitches, and Three-Quarter Stitches first; then add the Backstitch, French Knots, and Lazy Daisy Stitches. When stitching, bring the threaded needle up at 1 and all odd numbers and down at 2 and all even numbers.

Cross Stitch: Stitch the length of the row from left to right; then, stitch right to left *(Fig. 1)*.

Fig. 1

One-Quarter Stitch and **Three-Quarter Stitch:** Stitch 1-2 is the One-Quarter Stitch *(Fig. 2)*. When stitches 1-4 are stitched in the same color, the resulting stitch is called a Three-Quarter Stitch.

Fig. 2

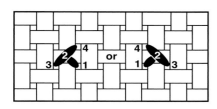

Backstitch: For outlines and details, Backstitch should be stitched after the design has been completed *(Fig. 3)*.

Fig. 3

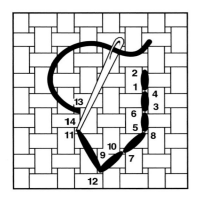

French Knot: Bring the needle up at 1. Wrap the floss twice around the needle. Insert the needle at 2, tighten the knot, and pull the needle through the fabric, holding the floss until it must be released *(Fig. 4)*.

Fig. 4

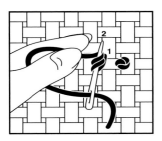

Lazy Daisy Stitch: Bring the needle up at 1 and make a loop. Go down at 1 and come up at 2, keeping the floss below the point of the needle *(Fig. 5)*. Pull the needle through and go down at 3 to anchor the loop, completing the stitch.

Fig. 5

Straight Stitch: Bring the needle up at 1; go down at 2 *(Fig. 6)*.

Fig. 6

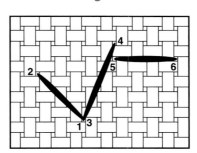

PROJECT FINISHING

Embroidery Hoop Frames
We finished the Penguin with Bell, Kitty, and Puppy in painted embroidery hoops with festive bows. You will need a 4" diameter wood embroidery hoop, a 16" length of 1" wide sheer ribbon, acrylic paint, clear acrylic spray sealer, craft glue, and a paintbrush.

Paint the embroidery hoop. When dry, spray with sealer. Center the design in the embroidery hoop; tighten the hoop. Trim the excess fabric even with back of hoop. Place craft glue on the cut edges of the stitched piece. Tie a ribbon bow. Glue the bow to the top of the stitched piece. Trim the ribbon ends.

Gift Tags
We finished the Modern Reindeer, Christmas Tree, and Holiday Ornaments as gift tags. You will need a 2⅝" x 5¼" purchased gift tag or use the pattern, page 32, to cut your own from cardstock. You will also need a ¼" hole punch (if making your own tag), baker's twine, glitter washi tape, and craft glue.

If necessary, punch a hole in the tag. Centering the design, trim the stitched piece to 2⅜" x 2⅞". Glue the stitched piece to the tag. Place a piece of washi tape across the tag above the stitched piece. Loop a piece of baker's twine through the tag hole.

Greeting Card

We finished the Candy Cane, Mitten, and Chimney Santa as handmade greeting cards. You will need a 5$\frac{1}{2}$" x 12" piece of cardstock and craft glue.

Centering the design, trim the stitched piece to 3$\frac{3}{4}$" x 3$\frac{3}{4}$". Crease and fold the card into three equal sections *(Fig. 7)*. Cut a 2$\frac{3}{4}$" x 2$\frac{3}{4}$" opening in the middle section *(Fig. 8)*. Centering the design, glue the stitched piece behind the opening. Fold the card; glue the left section over the wrong side of the stitched piece.

Fig. 7

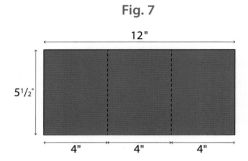

Fig. 8

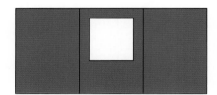

Ornament

We finished Santa's Sleigh, Happy Howl-a-days, and the Candle as ornaments. You will need a 3" x 3" piece of white mat board, $\frac{1}{2}$ yd of baby rickrack, craft glue, and straight pins.

Centering the design, trim the stitched piece to 5" x 5". Stretch the piece over the mat board and glue the edges to the back side. Using the straight pins to hold the rickrack in place until dry, glue the rickrack to the front edge of the stitched piece, forming a loop for hanging, folding the rickrack to turn the corners, and folding the cut ends to the back. Allow glue to dry and remove the pins.

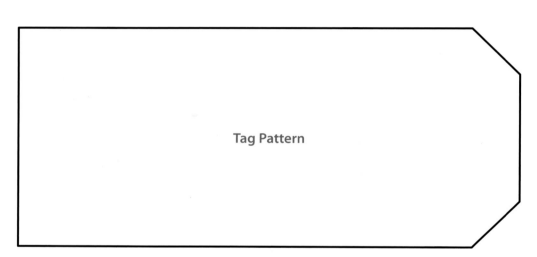

Tag Pattern

Production Team: Technical Writer – Lisa Lancaster; Technical Associate – Mary Sullivan Hutcheson; Contributing Associate – Kytanna McFarlin; Editorial Writer – Susan Frantz Wiles; Senior Graphic Artist – Lora Puls; Graphic Artist – Frances Huddleston; Contributing Graphic Artist – Maggie Adams; Photostylist – Lori Wenger; Photographer – Ken West.